Saint John of the Mall

SAINT JOHN OF THE MALL

Reflections for the Advent Season

Jon Swanson

ISBN-13: 978-1979688758

ISBN-10: 1979688753

Social Media Chaplain

3933 Hedwig Dr

Fort Wayne, IN 46815

Scripture taken from the Holy Bible, NEW INTERNATIONAL VERSION®, NIV®
Copyright © 1973, 1978, 1984, 2011 by Biblica, Inc.® Used by permission. All rights
reserved worldwide.

NEW INTERNATIONAL VERSION® and NIV® are registered trademarks of
Biblica, Inc. Use of either trademark for the offering of goods or services requires the
prior written consent of Biblica US, Inc.

Contents

Foreword

Two things have been consistent in my routine for the past couple of years. Early in the morning, I pour my cup of coffee and settle in at my computer to read Jon's daily devotional waiting in my email. I have known Jon for decades and was well aware that his writings were worth my time!

One December morning, Jon wrote about seeing a bearded man sitting near Starbucks at the mall. I was instantly drawn into the story. I knew that very spot and could easily visualize the scene.

After four days of reading, I knew I had to meet this man at the mall. I wanted to hear him speak the words of wisdom to me that he was sharing with Jon. With Jon's description of him, I knew he wouldn't be hard to find. I went to the mall and walked each corridor. I sadly concluded that Saint John was elsewhere that afternoon.

A few days later as I read, I made a discovery. The mall meetings with Saint John were in Jon's head, not at the mall. But I didn't feel foolish. I was captivated.

As the conversations between Saint John and Jon unfolded, I knew that I now had a guide for my Advent season. Amid the buying and wrapping and giving, Saint John's words have slowed my pace as I contemplate Christ's first coming, His life, and the yet-to-be-fulfilled promise of His second coming.

Thank you, Jon, for writing with the creativity that drew me into the story that has now become this book. But most of all, thank you for sharing the insights that Saint John brought to us about the One who became flesh to be my Savior.

Char Binkley
Fort Wayne, Indiana

Preface: About Saint John

The idea for this book arrived in October, 2015, about the same time Christmas decorations began to appear at our mall. That would have been fine if I didn't go to the mall. But Nancy and I walk at the mall when the weather gets cold. And the weather was cold.

As we walked, I had to fight the Christmas spirit. Or better, the competitive, commercial, consuming Christmas spirit. Like you, perhaps, I wanted to understand Christmas more calmly, more creatively, more expectantly. I decided to turn back to an old, churchy word: Advent.

For years, I've thought about Advent, the few weeks before Christmas. I'd seen Advent calendars, some with chocolates. I'd learned that Advent, as a season in the church calendar, wasn't really about the arrival of the baby Jesus. It was more about the return of the grown-up Jesus, the dead and risen Jesus, the back-to-heaven-coming-again Jesus. I wondered whether I would find Christmas more meaningful if I studied more about this big picture.

I realized that the Apostle John could be the perfect person to talk with about both advents, first and next. He had lived for years and years after the resurrection. He knew Jesus well. He had cared for Mary, the mother of Jesus, and had heard her stories.

Yep. I needed to talk to John.

And then one day I thought, "What if the old guy at the mall is Saint John?" Because there had been, for the past couple years, a man at the mall, always sitting on a bench when we showed up to walk. If I had to guess, I'd say he needed to get out of wherever he stays. And the mall is warm.

I realized that being stuck at the mall would be a little like being exiled on the Island of Patmos. And so I started writing about the conversations Nancy and I had with Saint John of the

Mall, as best as I could imagine them. I posted some at my blog, 300wordsaday.com, during December of 2015. In 2016, I filled in the gaps to provide a full 25 days of readings for the month of December.

I got a text from my friend Lee a few days after Christmas 2015. It was a photo from the fountain at the local mall and the comment, "I haven't seen John yet." I heard that from some other friends as well. Somehow, other people were reading these conversations as if I had found a real saint sitting at our mall.

So I'm not sure how to answer the question, "Did you really see Saint John of the Mall?" I'll leave that to you as you read.

Jon Swanson
November 2017

How to use an Advent reader

Advent is the season before Christmas.

On the historical church calendar, Advent includes the four Sundays before Christmas. On Advent calendars, it usually begins on December 1. This book follows that convention.

There's one reading for each day. On most days, there is also a passage from the Gospel of John which is related to the reading. At the back of the book are reflection questions and applications if you want to spend more time with the reading.

1

Saint John of the Mall

Nancy and I started walking at the mall a few winters back. It saved our lives.

That sounds dramatic, like walking kept us from a heart attack. For all we know, it has. But we started talking every day while we walked. Since then, we've weathered a variety of life events. Deaths of parents, job changes, kids in college, kids in weddings. We're still talking and walking.

Like I said, it saved our lives.

We were walking at the mall early one Black Saturday, two days after Thanksgiving. It was a way to avoid the crowds that would show up later. On our first lap, we saw a guy sitting on a bench not far from Starbucks. Just sitting. He had a white beard, but not the usual Christmas white beard. It had the look of necessity, not choice. And he was much thinner than the usual bearded holiday hero.

But his eyes.

I've seen the eyes of people who sit in the mall. There is

distractedness. There is pain. There is a sense of resignation or worry or lostness.

This man's eyes were different. There was an intensity. And affection.

He was looking into an empty section of the hallway as if he was looking at a friend or a holiday memory. It was a little scary, actually. I've seen that look in the eyes of people who were hallucinating. But when we were passing his bench, he glanced at us. And the eye contact made it clear: he was fully present.

We walked our second lap and stopped to get a cup of coffee to take home.

I knew the barista from years ago. She'd been one of my college students. We'd reconnected at the mall.

"Who is that guy? Do you know anything about him?" I asked.

Brenda laughed. "We call him Saint John of the Mall. I think you need to talk to him sometime."

2

Anticipating a Conversation

We have obligations most Sundays that keep us from the mall. So it wasn't until Monday morning that we went walking again. I looked for the man from Saturday. "Saint John of the Mall" Brenda had called him.

We started our walk at Red Robin. We tossed our coats on the bench near the door. At 7:00 on the Monday morning after the Thanksgiving holiday, there's not much concern about theft.

As we approached the center court of the mall, I started getting nervous. I never know how to start conversations with people I don't know.

He wasn't on his bench.

It's a big mall. I'm not sure why I expected him to be there, but I still wanted to know about him.

It made me think a little about anticipation.

I never was much of an Advent person as a kid. But back then, I looked forward to Christmas. Now, I don't. I became a pastor. I wore out from all the Christmas performing. Planning events, scheduling rehearsals, solving technical problems. We never got around to thinking about the family part of Christmas until after Christmas Eve.

I'll be accurate. *I didn't.* Nancy did. And she would pull me patiently into the gift process.

We started doing treasure hunts for our kids. We wrote some clues. Opening gift cards is a little more exciting when you have to find them.

One year, we sent our young-adult children to the mall. We hid clues in lockers, then hid the keys in other lockers. While other people wandered the mall wondering, our kids were following a calling.

What made the adventures interesting was the anticipation. They appreciated the gifts because of the process. They appreciated the process because it was pursued together.

That's what Advent is for the church, *a collective anticipation of the Kingdom of God.*

I was so wrapped up in my thoughts that I nearly tripped over a man's feet. I turned to apologize.

"My name is John," he said.

3

Incarnation

John 1:14

Saint John of the Mall wasn't where I expected him to be. He had been by the coffee place. I thought it was his regular place. My friend Brenda knew him, after all.

But here he was, sitting in front of The Children's Place. With his feet out. Where I could trip over them.

"They weren't in your way," he said. "You were so lost in thought that you almost stepped on me."

I turned to Nancy, looking for support. She shook her head. "You were somewhere else," she said. "It happens often so I'm used to it. But this time it got you into something."

No allies.

I turned back to John. "So are you sitting here because Christmas is about children?" I put just enough irony in my voice so no one listening would assume I was one of those holiday people.

John smiled at me. "I wouldn't start Christmas with children.

I'd start it with creativity, with the start of everything. Christmas isn't just about babies, not even baby Jesus."

I was pretty surprised.

He got up slowly and motioned Nancy and me to walk with him. He looked older than time, but he could still walk pretty well.

"Not that there wasn't a baby Jesus. It's just that the baby part wasn't the most amazing part. It was the flesh part. Baby, child, teen, adult. All the stages, all the moods, all the parties, all the arguments, all the words."

"So, shouldn't you be down by the Body Shop?" I asked. I laughed.

"It's closed," he said. "And the baby part *is* important. But Jesus put on a body and walked around. That's the amazing part. God walking and talking with people. Like me. Like you."

John looked up. We were by the maternity shop.

"I'll leave you here," he said. "My friends Matt and Luke like to tell baby stories as the starting point for Christmas. I'll wait for them here."

4

Not What He Seems

John 2:1-11

We went to the mall Saturday morning. After a busy week of people, the emptiness was refreshing. We found Saint John by the coffee shop. I asked him about Matt and Luke. He shook his head and muttered something about wisdom and following stars.

I pointed at Starbucks and asked if he needed coffee.

"I've never acquired the taste," he said. "I'm good with water most of the time. I used to drink a little wine, but somehow after you've had the best ever..."

He shook his head and was quiet.

I wasn't sure what to say. I admit, I'm capable of my own version of profiling. A man with somewhat ragged clothes, who sits at the mall before the stores open, has some kind of story. And in my conversations with people who look worn by life, that story sometimes includes self-medication. I usually wait for the story to come out.

He looked at me. "You are wondering whether I'm like the drunkards and sinners that Jesus was accused of hanging out with," he said.[1] It was a statement, not a question.

I shrugged. "I'm not sure I would use that language, but that is a way of saying it."

He laughed. It was a clean, clear, soul-clearing laugh. I don't know how else to describe it. Most laughs have some amount of sarcasm or ridicule or self-deprecation or however you would describe the laugh that comes when watching "America's Funniest Home Videos." This laugh was the opposite of all of those. It was a laugh of pure delight.

"I do hang out with Jesus," he said, "and I did. But wine was not what got me into trouble. And when I talk about the best wine ever, it wasn't exaggeration. If Jesus himself were to make wine, isn't that how you would describe it?"

1. In fact, Jesus himself was accused of being a drunkard by the Pharisees in Luke 7:34.

5

Andrew and John

John 1:35-40

I went to get coffee for Nancy and me to share. And a bottle of water for Saint John of the Mall.

Nancy is better than I am at asking questions about people's lives. They started talking. When I came back, she was just saying, "How did you start following Jesus?"

"I grew up on the lake," he said. "My family worked in the fishing industry. Had for generations. My older brother was taking over the business from my dad. My friend Andrew was in the same boat."

I winced. I waited for a laugh. Apparently, John isn't into puns.

"So we had time to discuss religion and politics and life. Andrew and I even were able to visit a distant cousin who lived in Jerusalem. He worked in the religious bureaucracy.[1] While we were there, we began spending time with another John. He was known for his open-air meetings. And for his attacks on the

---

1. After Jesus is arrested, we read that Peter and another disciple go to the High Priest's house. It's likely that the other disciple is John. See John 18:15-16.

bureaucracy. I didn't want to cause trouble for my cousin, so Andrew and I headed for home. We traveled with John. We were taking in his teaching. And one day our mentor introduced us to Jesus."

"You mean like told you about Jesus?" Nancy asked. "Or had you pray some kind of prayer?"

John shook his head. "Not like you mean. John pointed across the road and said, 'He's way more worthy of your attention than I am.' And so we went and met Jesus."

Nancy and I looked at each other. Was this old man at the mall saying he was THE Saint John?

He ignored us. "We followed Jesus home. Or to the place he was staying. And we were hooked. Andrew recruited his brother, Peter. My brother James got on board."

John sipped his water. Nancy and I were quiet.

This was getting interesting. And odd.

6

Saint John and the Best Coffee Ever

John 2:1-11

"But what about the wine?" I finally asked. "Before I left you were talking about the best wine ever."

Saint John smiled at me.

"Why are you so interested?" he finally said. "It's not like you are an expert."

I shook my head. The truth is, I've never had a glass of wine. Growing up, it was one of those things that the "true" followers of Jesus would never do. Just like dancing and movies and smoking and playing face cards. It wasn't like we had conversations about these things. We just didn't do them.

"It's curious," John said. "I've had the best wine ever served, the best wine never grown. And I'm expecting the best wine ever at the end of all things. And I lift a cup regularly in memory of that last supper and in anticipation of an amazing wedding feast. I was served by Jesus, and I remember Jesus. And you were told, for religious reasons, not to drink wine." John laughed. "You even make wedding toasts with coffee."

I looked down.

"Look at me," John said. "It's okay. You weren't wrong. But you were missing a couple of important points. First, the wine wasn't the main point, the relationships were. Jesus and his mother, his mother and the family, all of us with our friends having a great time. Jesus was part of the community."

"So laughing in community matters? More than I think?"

John smiled. "Of course it does. Why is a wedding feast the celebration of the end of all time and the beginning of the rest of forever?"

"Good question," I said. "So what's the second point."

"Take a look in your cup," he said.

I took the lid off my cup, expecting a miracle of some sort. It was still coffee.

"Of course it's coffee. I'm not making you change your convictions. Just like there is no rule that you must abstain, there's no rule that you must partake. Don't confuse liberty with relationship. But whichever you do, enjoy it. Jesus did great work even in small works, like wine at the end of a wedding."

John walked away. I relaxed a little about holiday rules. And I sipped the coffee.

It was different than the Christmas blend I had purchased earlier. This was the best coffee I've ever tasted. I lifted my cup to John's departing back.

"To the Groom," I said.

7

Saint John and the Cubs Fan

John 1:43-51

Early the next morning, Nancy and I walked past Arnie's Jerseys and Stuff. It's the local sports memorabilia store. We usually ignore it, not being fans of the teams, the old players, or the markups. This time I stopped, staring at the Ernie Banks Cubs uniform shirt. It was part of a display of Cubs items. After they won the World Series, everyone became a fan. But the price on the Banks jersey made me stop.

As I stared, I heard a voice behind us.

"Chicago fans are irrationally faithful. Just like my friend Nathanael."

It was Saint John.

"What do you mean?" I said.

"Year after year, Cubs fans kept watching for a winning season. They kept showing up to worship at Wrigley, even when there was no hope of a positive outcome to the season. People learned the names of players who would never wear rings, never hold pennants, never play baseball in November."

I grinned. "Billy Williams, Don Kessinger, Ernie Banks, Glenn Beckert, Randy Hundley, Ron S..."

John held up his hand. "You learned those when you were nine years old. How many more years after that before they won the World Series?"

"Forty-eight years."

"Irrationally faithful," he said. "Like Nathanael. We grew up together. He was looking for the Messiah, learning details, memorizing Torah, keeping the faith. But like you and the Cubs, I'm pretty sure Nathanael thought Messiah would never come."

"What makes you think that?" I asked.

"Because when Philip told him that Jesus was the Messiah, Nathanael pushed back. 'Can anything good come from Nazareth?' was his first question. Can anything of value come from where we grew up?"

"But if Nathanael was such a doubter, why did Jesus accept him?" As I said it, I realized that we talk about accepting Jesus, not the other way around.

John smiled.

"Jesus knew his heart, knew that Nathanael wanted to believe in someone. He just didn't want to be disappointed again. And Jesus knew that wasn't going to happen."

I looked at him, uncertain.

"Jesus was the certainty for irrationally faithful people. Nathanael's healthy skepticism about pretenders was grounded in a desire to be proven right."

"Like the people who wept when the 2016 Cubs won," I said.

John smiled. "Ah, but so much more."

8

Zeal

John 2:13-22

We went to the mall in the evening. It was a gamble. Some evenings the crowds are a little lighter, even during the Christmas season. Tonight wasn't one of those nights. We sat for a bit in the food court and watched people.

There were lines at Chick-fil-a, at the Thai food place, at the cheesesteak place. In front of each counter, sales people had sample trays offering toothpicked tastes, creating more congestion. Mothers and kids tried to weave their way through the lines on their way to the restrooms. It looked like a human loom.

Nancy turned to me to say something about the lack of consideration the hungry people had for the desperate people. From the next table, we both heard, "Imagine someone knocking the trays out of their hands and then climbing over the counters."

We started to laugh. Then we realized that it was Saint John.

He had a cup of water and a stack of Saltines. But he wasn't eating. He was watching a Burmese child pulling on mom's hand, almost panicking.

Immediately, John was in front of the little family, pushing through the crowd. We couldn't see them, but we could see a path.

After a bit, John came back.

"Did anyone get hurt?" Nancy asked, smiling.

John shook his head. "I had no interest in hurting anyone. But I did have a strong interest in getting that child where he needed to go."

"Did that have something to do with your comment about knocking the trays down?" I asked. "Because that sounded a little like Jesus pushing around the vendors in the temple."

"People always think that was about the vendors extorting," John said. "But it wasn't. They were doing an acceptable business helping people have what they needed to worship. It's just that the place they were doing business was also the place where the women and former gentiles were trying to worship."

I must have looked lost.

"According to the rules, gentiles couldn't go into the temple itself. So they stood in the lobby to pray, trying to focus. And the people who could go further treated this space as a place to do business with others, not God."

John smiled.

"Jesus didn't get angry often. But when people desperate for God couldn't get to him..."

I finished his thought. "Jesus cleared the path no matter what it took or cost."

9

Saint John and the Man in the Corner

John 3:1-21

Nancy and I learned years ago that there are mall-walking regulars, people who show up at the same time every day. There's a sense of community when you wave at the same people every morning.

The other day, we got to the mall early. It was going to be a busy day. As expected, we saw a different group of people walking. The man with the Santa hat. The three wise women. And we saw Saint John, sitting in a corner of the food court.

We could barely see him, actually. We were on the upper level, and he was on the lower. He looked deep in conversation with someone.

When we came around the balcony on our second lap, we took the stairs down, to get a little more exercise. Honestly, though, I was curious about John. As we walked toward the food court, I recognized the well-dressed business leader walking away.

He has a good reputation in town, but I didn't expect to see him this early, at the mall, talking to someone as scruffy as Saint John.

John was walking, too. When he saw us, he stopped.

"Early morning counseling session?" I said, smiling.

"Not quite," John said. "More of a story-telling session. People ask me questions about stuff they hear on the news or things they wonder about. I listen, and then I say, 'Can I tell you something I heard from Jesus?'"

"And they listen?" I said. I've tried telling people what Jesus said. It almost never works.

"Of course they listen," John said. "They started the conversation. And I don't tell people what Jesus said as if I'm scolding. As I just told you, I say, 'Can I tell you something I heard from Jesus?'"

"You said that to him?" I said, looking at the man who had left.

"Of course. He was thinking about the loneliness coming from having to know all the answers. And about the deep fear he has about failing everyone and being shamed. It's why we met in a corner away from everyone. And I said, 'Can I tell you something I heard from Jesus? He was talking to a man almost like you, a leader named Nicodemus. He said, 'God didn't send his son to condemn the world, but so the world could be rescued through him.'"

"What did he say?" I asked.

"He said, 'If that's true, I'd give up trying to measure up. I'd quit.'"

John smiled. "I told him, 'that's exactly what I did when I left my business and followed Jesus.'"

10

Saint John and John

John 3:22-30

"I bet John the Baptist wasn't a fan of Christmas," I said to Saint John.

Nancy and John stopped and stared at me.

The three of us had been walking quietly through the mall. I'd been thinking about John's conversation with the community leader. I remembered that John the Baptist was mentioned right after Nicodemus in one of the stories about Jesus. And I started thinking about John's rustic approach to food and dress and social structures. It seemed completely at odds with everything we saw and smelled as we walked through the mall.

"John wasn't a grinch you know," John said. Which made Nancy and me stare at him.

"John was one of the most positive people I ever knew," John said. "And one of the most humble. He couldn't have been a fan of Christmas, since that wasn't invented as a holiday for centuries.

But he was completely sold out to the advent, to the anticipation of the coming of the Messiah."

"But he seems like an irrelevant wacko," I said. "The kind who stands in the parking lot and hollers at passing cars."

John laughed at me. "You read all the time about the importance of focus. John's life was built around getting everyone ready for the start of the festivities. Like one of your minimalists, he trained himself to eat the food available in the wild, honey and locusts. He contented himself with durable, obtainable clothing. And then he spent his time on preaching and baptizing."

"So I'll give you the focus," I said. "But it still sounds like the shouting guy."

"Don't use your metaphors to understand John," John said. "Use his. More than reacting to him, people responded to him and his message of a new life, a new hope, relief from the nagging burden of not measuring up to the human rules. And when his followers got jealous of the growing crowds around Jesus, John pointed them to a wedding."

John stopped. I realized that we were in front of Louie's Tux Shop. He pointed to the group of guys standing inside. Everyone was a little uncomfortable, facing one guy who had to be the groom.

Everyone but the guy in the torn jeans. He stood behind the groom, helping him try on jackets. When they found the right one, the jeans guy helped the rest of the guys find their suits, their accessories. When everyone was ready, it was hard to tell who had the biggest smile, the groom, or his friend.

John turned to me. "John said that he was the friend. His job was to get everything ready for the groom. His success came when he could get out of the way, when the crowds all showed up for the wedding."

We started walking again.

"I'm not sure whether he would have loved Christmas, but John loved Jesus." John's voice cracked a little. "And he was thrilled when he helped me put on a tux."

11

Saint John and the Manicure

John 4:1-29

I might have mentioned that we start our mall walks by a burger place called "Red Robin." The parking is close to the door and closest to our house.

I understand the irony of worrying about parking when you are going to walk.

About half a mile away, at the far end of the mall, is a little manicure shop. I've never been inside, mind you, but when you walk past a place 3-4 times a day for seven winters, you start to notice.

And on this morning, that's where Saint John was sitting. The gate covering the store entrance wasn't open. John was sitting on the bench in front of the door, talking to one of the workers. I think she had arrived early, and John just sat down next to her.

I was worried, a little. I mean if he was THE Saint John, it couldn't be good for his reputation to be sitting in a dark hallway talking to a young woman. Especially someone who, judging by her accent, wasn't born in this country.

Not that I was eavesdropping. Not that I was judging. I was just curious.

John saw us walking by. He waved us over.

"I want you to meet my friend," he said. "We were just talking about Christmas. She was asking me whether it was better luck to have a real tree or an artificial tree. She wondered what my ancestors had done. I told her that I didn't know how to answer that. What about you?"

"My ancestors lived on a farm by the woods," I said. "They always had real trees. I never thought about luck. But it did feel more Christmasy."

Saint John smiled. "Can I tell you what Jesus said in a conversation like this? A woman said that her ancestors worshiped on one mountain and that Jesus' ancestors worshiped on another one. And she wanted to know which was best."

The woman looked at John intently. "What did this Jesus say?"

"He said that worshipers don't have to worry about a place and an altar and offerings. He said that the Father God is looking for people who will worship in spirit and in truth."

"Even people like me?" she asked. "People sitting at the edge of the crowd?"

"Especially," John said. "Jesus loved those of us at the edges."

12

Saint John Looks at Love and Gifts

John 4:43-54

We found Saint John of the Mall sitting in front of the gift wrapping store. It's not really a buying and selling store. That store closed. The Rescue Mission uses the space, wrapping gifts and accepting contributions.

It was early. No one was around. We sat next to John and looked through the window at the wastepaper baskets full of scraps.

"It was crazy busy in there yesterday," John said. "I sat here all day watching people carry stuff in, get it wrapped, and carry it out. Most people were looking intense or distracted. Ready to be done or ready to keep going. Almost no one smiled."

"Shopping is pretty intense," Nancy said. "You want to get the thing that matches what the person wants."

"Which is why we went to gift cards and cash," I said.

John leaned forward and looked at us both. "I think there must be a standard relationship conversation that says, 'If you buy me that gift, I'll know that you love me.'"

We both shook our heads.

"Not you two," John said. "Or your kids. But isn't it possible that something close to that happens in lots of houses, lots of relationships?"

He stood up. We started walking. "Once, Jesus was visiting friends in a small town. He wasn't from there, but he'd been at a wedding there. As we walked down the street, a couple of servants waved at him. They knew, though many people didn't, that Jesus was responsible for the water turning into wine at that wedding.

"A wealthy man came from Jesus' new hometown, a few miles away. He wanted Jesus to come and heal his son who was dying.

"Jesus said, 'people are always asking for wonders before they believe.'"

I smiled. "That's a lot like 'if you buy me this gift, I'll know that you love me.'"

John nodded. "What was so powerful was that the man didn't argue about the characterization. He simply said, 'Sir, come down before my child dies.' And Jesus said, 'Go, your son will live.' The man went. The son lived."

I asked the question that was in both of our hearts. "But what about all the people since then who have made that same request without the same result?"

Saint John looked at us. I'm not sure I've ever seen such compassion in someone's eyes. And he waited for awhile.

"I know that's not a theoretical question," he finally said. "Even after all these years you still miss your daughter. And I know this. That you didn't decide God's love depended on the particular gift."

He walked on and left us to sit. Remembering the healing that hadn't happened. And the love we have still known.[1]

---

1.   Kathryn Anne Swanson was born July 28, 1989 and died September 1, 1989. You can read more in the epilogue of *Lent for Non-Lent People*.

13

Saint John by the Fountain

John 5:1-15

There's a fountain at our mall. During the day, the fountain runs, keeping the reflecting pool around it stirred up. There are always people sitting on the benches around the pool, waiting for something. Or someone. Kids toss coins into the pool, which are gathered and given to Habitat for Humanity and the Rescue Mission. You could say it is a healing kind of fountain.

Early in the morning, the fountain is quiet. The benches are mostly empty, except for a couple guys who wait for walking buddies. And this morning, Saint John of the Mall. The fountain is three-fourths of the way around our path. I'd been wondering if John was at the mall this morning. We didn't see him until we stopped at the blood pressure machines which face the water. As I sat there, I noticed John, talking with one of the men. The man's cane was resting on the bench next to him.

Our blood pressure was fine. We walked toward John and the man. I heard John say, "Do you want to get well?"

The man talked about how long his knee had been hurting. He talked about how hard it was to get a doctor to listen. He talked about how much work it was to get help. He talked about a friend who dragged him along to the mall, just to get out of the house.

John asked him again: "Do you want to get well?"

I thought the man was tired of being picked on, so I walked up to them and greeted John. He introduced us to the man, Jakov. John said, "I'll be back after a bit. Think about my question." And then he started walking with us.

"We overheard your conversation," I said. "Do you ever get frustrated when people make excuses rather than answering you? I mean, what would happen if he demonstrated a little faith? Wouldn't you want to heal him then?"

I was thinking about the time that Jesus healed a man by a pool. And the time that Peter and John healed a man after Jesus had ascended.

John scowled at me, just for a moment. "You don't know the text very well. Both of those times, people were healed without any great belief at all. The only thing they did was to look up at the person talking with them. Healing's not a reward for faith."

We walked for a bit.

John started to smile, slowly. "In fact, I'll say to you what Jesus told that man he healed. 'Stop sinning.' It's what he usually said after he healed people. As if the physical healing was what the people cared most about, and the relationship with God was what Jesus cared most about."

14

Expectations and Expectancy

John 5:39

Nancy and I were talking about why we don't care for Christmas. We realized that it's about the expectations. There are scheduling expectations, there are emotional expectations, there are gifting expectations. There are even expectations about not getting caught up in the expectations.

"Help," I said to Saint John. "Can you sort out the struggle with expectations?"

I asked him because John is a pretty good person to talk with about expectancy. John grew up in Malachi-shaped Israel, expecting a prophet like Elijah.[1] He found that prophet when he met John the Baptist who talked about expecting someone else. He followed the one John the Baptist pointed him toward, expecting the kingdom to be established by Jesus. He expected the resurrection of Jesus. He was told to expect the return of the

---

1.   Malachi 4:5-6.

king, first by Jesus, then again as he wrote down the words of Revelation. John's whole life was about expectations.

"There's a difference between *expectations* and *expectancy*," John said. "Jesus almost never lived up to expectations. In fact, he was talking to the religious leaders one day. It was right after the healing we talked about yesterday. He talked to them about how they were ignoring all the things that pointed to him. And he said, 'You search the Scriptures because you think that in them you have eternal life; and it is they that bear witness about me, yet you refuse to come to me that you may have life.'"[2]

John started laughing as he was quoting Jesus. "Imagine going to people who are seminary trained, who have memorized the Bible, who have staked their careers on their religious pursuit of telling people how to measure up and saying, 'I do not think that word means what you think it means.'"

I must have looked worried. John put his hand on my shoulder. "There were lots of people who heard the words and connected them to Jesus. That's what I mean by the difference between expectations and expectancy. The religious leaders lived by expectations, and Jesus didn't measure up. But others lived in expectancy. We were waiting for a person who would fulfill the promises, who would bring hope and healing. We were pretty sure that Isaiah was pointing to someone real when he quoted,

'The Spirit of the Lord God is upon me,
because the Lord has anointed me
to bring good news to the poor;"[3]

And then John forgot he was talking to me. He slipped into Hebrew while he was quoting Isaiah. But that was okay. Expectancy can do that. Living in the freedom of hope rather than the chains of expectations can let you forget where you are.

2. John 5:39-40.
3. Isaiah 61:1-2.

15

Saint John and the Christmas Performance

John 5:44

"Can we go back to talking about expectations?" I said.

John had pointed to the whole "meaning of Christmas" perspective, to the expectancy of the one bringing good news to the poor. But it didn't solve a struggle that I kept having. I was still wrestling with the practical implications of doing stuff at Christmas.

"Go ahead," John finally said. I realized that I had been so caught up in my thoughts that I forgot the people walking with me.

"Sorry," I said, shaking my head to clear my thoughts.

"I think most of the reason I don't care for Christmas is spending so many Christmas seasons getting ready for events at church. Christmas programs. Advent series. Christmas Eve services. It often feels like I can't stop to think about Christmas, about Christ, until after the last event on Christmas Eve. And by then, it's too late."

Nancy nodded. "Even when he's home, he's thinking ahead to the next event, the next performance. Sometimes I think that the only way he's really home for Christmas IS in his dreams."

John thought for a bit. "I think that the word that's got you trapped is the word 'performance.' Somewhere, you got caught up in performing for Christmas, and it's taken the place of celebrating Christmas. The deep, honest, participation in joy and grief and people."

He laughed. "I think Jesus was talking about you one day. In that conversation where Jesus talked about the religious leaders ignoring the scriptures that pointed to him, Jesus said, 'How can you believe if you accept praise from one another, yet you make no effort to obtain the praise that comes from the only God?'"

"I thought I was thinking about God," I said. "I mean, as a third grader with a fourth grade part in the Christmas program, was I really getting the kind of praise confused?"

John stopped and looked at me with his clear, piercing eyes. "All those years, how often were you thinking about participating *with* people, and how often were you performing *for* people?"

He and Nancy walked on. They had their own conversation.

I stood in the middle of the crowd for a very long time.

16

Saint John and the Geography Lesson

John 1:9-14

I got a note from a friend. She'd been visiting the mall late one evening. She said that she had looked for Saint John but missed him, "though we didn't go through the Macy's or Penney's mattress departments where I assume he sleeps."

I hadn't thought about that.

"Rabbi, where are you staying?" I said when we saw him next.

"Not here," he said.

He gave me an address.[1]

We talked about the importance of geography for people. "Where do you live?' is a question we ask often. I think it's a way of sorting people. If we know where they are from, we can anticipate how they will think and act.

"Nathanael discounted Jesus because he was from Nazareth," I

---

1.   This is how John and Andrew asked Jesus about where he was staying in John 1.

said. "And you, I mean, the disciples were very hesitant about the woman in Samaria."

John nodded. "For good or ill, every group of people tends to evaluate every other group of people from somewhere else. In fact, that tendency is at the heart of Advent."

"No room in the inn?" I said, hesitantly.

John shook his head. "Don't get wrapped up in the little details of Christmas," he said with a gentle firmness. "Advent is the expectation of deliverance, of royal peace, of holy authority. 'The Word became flesh and made his dwelling among us.' It's more than the story of a wandering couple or a transient rabbi."

"It's the construction company's owner moving into the city he just built?" I said, anxious to offer a new metaphor.

"No, it's the true light that gives light to everyone finally coming into the world," John said. "Not everyone recognized him at first. But slowly we did. And by his light, we saw that he was part of a geography completely different than ours, yet ours was part of his."

John stopped.

"You get consumed by today's details. You need to keep the whole story in mind." And he walked into a store. I looked up at the sign.

"Things Remembered."

17

Camping with Saint John

John 15:9-17

That evening, we went to the address John had given us. As I thought, it wasn't a house. It was a campground not far from the mall. The sign said that it was closed, but even from the parking lot I could see a couple of tents attempting, unsuccessfully, to hide from view. And a small fire.

And John.

He was sitting by the fire, like he was the one keeping it burning.

We were a hundred yards away, of course, so I couldn't see details. But I knew it was John. There's something about the way he carries himself. Confident without being arrogant.

We sat in the car. It was warm. And I wanted to see what was happening.

A young couple crawled out of one of the tents. She was

expecting. Another guy crawled out of the other tent. They walked toward the fire.

Apparently John had a pot in the fire. He reached for a bowl or something, filled it, and handed it to her. John took another bowl and filled it for one of the guys.

John stood up. He looked across the empty campground, across the parking lot, straight at us. He tilted his head in what may have been a nod. And turned back toward the fire and the young people and spread out his arms, just for a moment. And they all sat down.

We left, not saying a word. A little later, I heard Nancy whispering. "God, hide them in your hand." After some recent stories about homeless camps being cleared out, I understood her fear.

When I asked him about it a couple days later, all he said was, "as I have loved you, so you must love one another."

That night, we put some blankets in the car and went back to the campground. It was empty. "Loving one another is going to take some looking," I said.

18

Breaking Bread with Saint John

John 6:1-13

Nancy and I needed to do some Christmas shopping. We decided to head to the food court at the mall for supper and then shop. There's a new Thai place, so we shared a plate with two entrees and rice.

"You eat like you haven't had anything for a couple days," said the person at the next table. I looked up. I had been so focused on our meal that I hadn't noticed Saint John. He had a cup of water and a small piece of bread or roll.

"It's from the sub place," he said. "They often share a bit of food with me. I don't eat much."

"That broken piece of bread in the middle of a crowd," I said. "It seems familiar."

Nancy agreed. "Everyone seated in family groups. People in the same place looking for meaning in a chaotic culture."

John smiled at us. "So, how many people do you think there are here? A thousand?"

I shook my head. "I have no sense of numbers of people. But maybe. There's enough noise for a thousand people or more."

"Imagine several times this many people sitting around on the ground, and Jesus teaching. The only noise is his voice, and then the whispered sound of people passing on what they heard."

Nancy smiled. "That many people concentrating on what Jesus said. The sense of community must have been amazing."

John shook his head. "I'd love to let you think that, but the people didn't all agree with Jesus. In fact, many little clusters hoped that he agreed with *them*. Like the people sitting around us today. Some are hoping their gift will restore a relationship. Others are hoping it will make someone jealous. Some are looking for the least they can give to keep the peace."

"That sounds pretty cynical," I said. I was pretty sensitive to Christmas skepticism. I have years of practice.

"I'm just being accurate," John said. "Within a couple days, most of that crowd walked away from Jesus. He didn't fit with their idea of a leader. He had his own plan and wasn't planning to fit with theirs.

"But some were paying attention. The twelve were pretty focused on what he was saying."

I pointed to the hunk of bread in front of him. "I thought that there was some debate about how to feed the crowd."

John smiled. "There was. Andrew, my earliest friend following Jesus, entertained the idea that Jesus might provide for the whole crowd faster than Chick-fil-a could cater. The rest of the group wasn't sure. But when we passed out fish and it kept coming, and when we each ended up with a big basket of leftovers, we were pretty focused."

"I'm guessing that you weren't focused on the food?" I asked.

"When you are part of the process of a miracle, you don't focus on the outcome," he said. "You focus on the one who blessed the bread. And your hands."

19

What Did Jesus Say That Day

John 6

Nancy and Saint John and I were sitting in the food court, talking about the story of the feeding of the 15,000. That's what I call it.

"Maybe you can help me," I said to John. "I have a couple questions about the version of the story we read in 'The Gospel according to Saint John.' I'm guessing that talking to you is as good a chance as any to get answers."

He smiled. "I'll do what I can, though it's almost like talking to yourself."

I ignored him. "First question: why doesn't the gospel of John, or any of the other gospels, tell us what Jesus was teaching about that day? We learn about what happened at the end of the day, but we don't even get an outline."

"You need to read closer," John said. "He had compassion, he talked about the kingdom of God, and he healed. But you need to understand. The Twelve had been on an internship for a few weeks. As soon as we got back, Jesus headed for the wilderness and was met by this huge crowd. None of the disciples were interested in taking notes. Not nearly as much as talking about what had been happening."

I shook my head. "So the Twelve were more interested in themselves than in recording teachings for us?"

John laughed. "You could read it that way, I suppose. But if you actually took the time to read the whole story, you would see that the crowd scene is tied to a long teaching about being the bread of life. Jesus gives a physical example by feeding everyone, and then explains it."

"But what was he saying?"

"I think you'd be surprised by how much of the teaching you would know. Jesus often taught the same ideas many times to different groups of people."

"Okay," I said. "That helps. But I have another question."

John leaned back to wait.

20

On Bread and Water

John 6

"Second question: why did Jesus avoid being made king by the crowd? Isn't that what he came for?"

Saint John of the Mall leaned forward.

"That's a good question, and fairly simple to answer. They wanted to make Jesus king by force. They wanted to make him king rather than coming under his kingship and into his kingdom."

"Could you explain that a little more," Nancy said.

"All the time people are trying to make Jesus be their kind of king," John said. "They want to force him into leadership. They want to force kingdoms to accept him. It is happening in your day, too. But Jesus will only be king on his terms. It's why he told us to pray that his kingdom would come on earth in the same way that it is in heaven. The people wanted a bread king. He's a people king."

"Okay, third question," I said. "Why doesn't the Gospel of John talk about Peter walking on the water? Is it professional jealousy? Is it because no one else had the courage to step out of the boat? Because there are sure a lot of sermons about how we are supposed to step out of the boat in faith."

John leaned back. "You know, the Holy Spirit was involved in reminding the writers of what had happened. The story is shaped by that direction. And that little glimpse of Peter wasn't the most important thing that happened that day. In fact, in that moment, it may be that the most important picture is that the twelve were working really hard, making no progress against wind and waves that resisted them. And in that moment, Jesus came. First appearing so faint as if a ghost. But then, tangible and powerful. Peter's story is merely one example of how fear becomes bravado becomes faith becomes fear becomes the presence of God. There were eleven other examples in that boat."

John stood up. "He still does that. Appears faintly, but always faithfully."

21

Saint John and the Brothers

John 7:1-9

There were four shopping days until Christmas. Anticipation was building at the mall. And it wasn't the good kind. As soon as the mall opened at 8 a.m., there were people moving through the halls with an intensity fueled by coffee and the office white elephant gift competition. And in the late evening, when Nancy and I usually can find some space to walk, children who should have been doing homework were dragging parents from store to store.

It all made me a little cranky.

"That place should be sued for false advertising," I said. Saint John looked where I was pointing. It was a greeting card shop. He looked back at me, one gray eyebrow raised.

"If you looked at the cards in there, you would find images of Christmas that are full of smiling families living together and laughing together and loving each other all the time. But the people we meet as we are walking aren't laughing, especially this week."

John laughed. "Around holidays, the worst always comes out. And there are no perfect families, where everyone believes the best and trusts each other. In fact, Jesus was human enough to be part of a family without them acknowledging who he was."

We slowed down. There were three teens in our way. They looked like brothers. One was looking at a jewelry display. As we moved past them, we heard the comments: "I'm guessing what she really wants for Christmas is a new boyfriend, not a new necklace."

John turned toward us to talk. "This one time, James and the rest of the brothers grabbed Jesus almost like that. They teased him about going to Jerusalem for the feast, to build his audience. At the time, they really didn't understand who he was."

"I've always thought that if we could really see Jesus," I said, "we'd have an easier time believing him."

John laughed. "Belief isn't about the facts you see. It's about the way you look at them."

22

Saint John and Looking For Jesus

John 7:1-52

Three days before Christmas and everyone is stuck. Not everyone, but those of us who want to get the perfect gift and yet have no idea who the person really is.

So you guess.

Maybe they will like this. Maybe they are interested in that.

I asked John.

"You get to know them," he said. "You listen to them. You take time to think about who they are rather than who you want them to be."

"But that takes time," I said. "And we only have three days to figure this out. What's the harm in guessing?"

"Depending on the person, there is much harm possible," he said. "A few months before Jesus' death, people were arriving at conclusions about who he was. And when you read through the story, it's hilarious. Just listen to what people were saying:

He is a good man.

He deceives the people.

How did he get such learning?

You are demon possessed.

Have the authorities decided he's the messiah?

We know where he's from. He couldn't be the messiah.

When the messiah comes, could he do any more than this man?

Will he go to visit the émigré Jews?

Will he teach the Greeks?

This is the prophet.

This is the messiah.

We can't arrest him, he speaks truth."

I started laughing at the list. "That gives me theological whiplash," I said. "That's amazing. What did Jesus say?"

"Throughout that time, he was simply saying who he was. But because they were listening to him a phrase at a time and not a paragraph at a time, they were getting distracted, getting stuck."

"I'm guessing that each one of those descriptions of Jesus could take you to a different way of living," I said.

John nodded. "Just like deciding what to buy someone, you need to listen to their heart rather than just yours."

23

The Messiah Sheep

$$\infty$$

John 10:1-18

Two days til Christmas and the mall was congested all the time. Now that school was out, kids were with their parents. Many were "stabled" in the play place. From time to time, a kid would stand up and look around. An adult would speak a name. The kid would turn toward the voice, get oriented, and go back to playing.

I had been watching the kids while I was waiting for Nancy. The women's room was congested, too.

"My sheep listen to my voice; I know them, and they follow me," said a voice next to me.[1] I laughed.

"They look a little like sheep," I said to Saint John. Because that's who it was. "Though it feels a little more like, 'All we like sheep have gone astray.'"

I started humming. It was the bass part from "All We Like Sheep." It's a movement in Handel's *Messiah*. For its blend of music and lyric, it's probably my favorite movement. I had attended a performance this year for the first time in decades. I've

---

1.   John 10:27.

been so busy with church stuff, body and mind and soul, that I haven't had the time or attention to stop and listen.

Actually, we attended a dress rehearsal. It meant that we could listen to the chorus pieces and didn't have to listen through all the solos. Our daughter, Hope, is in the chorus. That's why we could attend the rehearsal.

As we were listening to the chorus and the orchestra rehearse, and the directions from the conductor, I realized that it's more fun to participate in the *Messiah* than to simply listen. To be part of something that demands focus and awareness of those around you and willing obedience to the directions of the conductor.

"My sheep listen to my voice; I know them, and they follow me," John repeated.

"You said that," I scolded. Then I stopped. "Was Jesus talking about an orchestra?"

I knew he wasn't, but the idea of following a conductor was giving me a new picture of the sheep images. We, like sheep, have gone astray, and the Lord has laid on Him the iniquity of us all. When we listen to his voice, like sheep we can be led beside still water.

"I think this year, listening to the *Messiah* was part of restoring my soul." I finally said.

"My sheep listen to my voice; I know them, and they follow me," John said again. "Listening to the Messiah is always part of restoring your soul."

24

Waiting With Saint John

John 11:1-45

I headed to the mall alone on Christmas Eve morning. I wasn't there to walk. I had last-minute arrangements to make. And I wasn't alone. The mall was already full.

I stopped by the fountain. The crowded tension was stifling.

"Sit down," a familiar voice said. I turned and saw Saint John pointing at the space on the bench. "I need to tell you a story."

"The kids will be at the house soon," I said. "I don't have much time."

"I don't either," John said. "Sit down."

I sat down.

"Jesus was teaching one day, same as usual. 'Master,' a familiar voice said. It was one of the people who helped out around Martha's house. We wondered why this servant was here, two days journey from Bethany. 'Martha and Mary would like you to come,' he said. 'Lazarus, your friend is very sick.'

"Jesus loved that family. He should have moved immediately. But he didn't. Later it was clear that he loved them so much that he didn't move.

"A couple days later, somehow, he knew that Lazarus was dead. Then he decided to go. Some reminded him that he, and they, could be killed within a couple miles of Jerusalem. But he went anyway.

"When he arrived, he talked with Martha. Then he talked with Mary. He wept with Mary, in fact. And then he stood in the graveyard for a bit."

John stopped.

I waited expectantly. Finally, I said, "And then he called Lazarus out of from dead. Finish the story. Don't leave me waiting."

When John finally spoke, his voice was the gentlest it had been.

"You've been trying to understand Advent, looking ahead to the coming of Jesus. That was Martha and Mary. First looking ahead to the coming of Jesus, then lamenting to him his lack of action. But before there was the miracle, there was the presence.

"The people Jesus loves deeply still get scared and hurt and desperate. They go places that make them fear for their lives, and some of them die. And when he finally shows up too late, the people he loves tell him so, to his face. He listens, he weeps with them.

"For Mary and Martha, the presence of Jesus before the healing of Lazarus was barely enough. They were hardly holding on. But they did. In the face of the ridicule of those around, and the deep pain in their hearts, they held on. Something about being able to talk with him, weep with him, look to him. And the preview they got of the end of all things was amazing."

John smiled, as if he was remembering something.

"Yes, the end will be worth waiting for."

25

Christmas

The mall is closed today. I'm not sure where John is. I'll be at the hospital. I'm expecting to see him listening to patients, understanding their fear, offering them hope. I'm expecting to hear him talking with family members who are watching for any movement at all. I'm expecting to be reminded to love like Jesus loved.

But I expect that you may see him, too. He's the guy simply and clearly pointing past the decorations. Past the miracles of the moment to the One who does the work.

A friend of mine said that his Christmas is always rough. But, he said, "some people have reason to smile and that's good."

So for those of you who have reason to smile, that's good. Smile well today.

For those of you who have reason to weep, I'm sorry. Weep well today.

And for those of you like me, who can get a little out of sorts just for the effect, let's pick a side. As Paul said when writing to a group of people who faced the struggles of being human and following God, weep with those who weep, rejoice with those who rejoice. And long for the healing of all things.

I would say, "Christmas wishes from our family" but I have no idea what that means. But the people I'm most grateful to be a part of are grateful that you are part of us. Because we talk about you all the time.

26

Saint John and the Books

John 21:25

It was the day after Christmas. Saint John of the Mall was sitting in front of Barnes and Noble. Through the doorway we could see piles of books on tables. Every table had a sign: "Best books of 2016" and "Making the most of 2017" and "Clearance."

"All those stories," I said. "All that creativity. All those shelves. All those books."

"You know," John said, "if you took every conversation and comment that Jesus made, every action and miracle that Jesus did, and you started writing them out, they'd fill all these shelves."

And then he caught himself. "Maybe not. There are a lot more books now than when he talked. A lot more noise."

"A lot more clutter?" I said.

"Maybe," John said. "But not everything that has been written since then is clutter. Some of it actually brings clarity. And Jesus said that he was sending the Holy Spirit to teach and remind us of what Jesus had said. So not everything written is clutter."

I waited for him to mention my writings. But he didn't.

"But some of what is written about Jesus and his life and his words doesn't help," he said. "When you look at the Gospel of John, you find the idea of editing – selecting some materials and not others – for a purpose. There were many words, many signs, many conversations that Jesus had. There could have been a comprehensive catalog, but, as you read, 'these are written that you may believe that Jesus is the Messiah, the Son of God, and that by believing you may have life in his name.'"

I looked at him. "So the gospel isn't a newspaper? There is bias in the writing?"

John smiled. "The gospel writers weren't historians. Not even Luke. They were witnesses, giving accounts of the birth and life and death and life again of Jesus. Enough witness to give an account. Enough teaching to live a life. Enough Jesus to reveal hope for the future."

"It's funny," I said. "I wanted to talk with you about returns, about all the people bringing Christmas presents back today because they weren't quite right after all the expectations. But you are saying that Christmas never was about satisfied expectations."

"I never knew anything about Christmas," John said. "My life is all about advent. The first advent was about expecting a messiah. And the second advent, the one you and I share, has been about expecting the Messiah again. I gave up thinking that stuff would satisfy my expectations. But you know, knowing the one I'm expecting is pretty satisfying."

I closed my eyes to figure that out. When I opened them, the bench was empty.

But I'm glad he's been here this year. Advent seemed a little less frantic.

Epilogue

I keep having arguments in my head about where to look next for Saint John of the Mall.

I can't decide where to look when it's time to think about Jesus washing the disciples' feet. Because the obvious place to look is the big fountain, outside J.C. Penney. I found him there once before. But when I think about foot-washing, I suddenly think about the manicure place. And the idea of walking in and expecting someone else to take care of your feet. And finally looking over the top of the magazine and discovering that it's Jesus.

I try to figure out which of the eyeglass stores to find him in front of when I want to talk about the blind man that Jesus healed. Because there's an optical place. And there's a sunglasses store. And either of those would allow for a clever twist of the story.

But I think that now John is at J.C. Penney, watching the man ringing the bell by the Salvation Army kettle. He's a man who is trying to be helpful, working minimum wage, ringing a bell so that other people can have a shot at Christmas. The bell triggers tips as the shoppers rush home with their treasures.

And then John says, "You laugh about the rushing shoppers, but where is your bell?"

I start to look for him so we can talk about the time that Jesus got into a debate with religious people and they wanted to stone him. And I figured that it would happen by the TVs in Sears. Because Jesus could get into an argument with someone about the false religion of sport.

And John's not there. But as I walk out of Sears, I see him at one of the little tables by Auntie Anne's. He's leaning across the table listening to a young couple. I recognize them from one of the Dead Sea spa carts. I try to get past those carts without making eye contact. But here's John, listening to questions, explaining something.

As I walk toward them, I hear him say something about Abraham's hope. He looks up at me and warns me away with a shake of the head.

And I realize that Saint John has conversations with people whom I can never predict in places that I can't control. And I realize that he's not available for trivial pursuits. Pretty much like his friend Jesus.

When you talk to him next, if you see him at the mall, would you tell him that I said "hello"?

Because I'm almost sure you'll be seeing him.

26 Questions for Reflection and Discussion

Whether you are reading Saint John alone or with other people, sometimes questions can help you think through the story. Here is a question for every day of this book.

1. Can you think of a time when you imagined that someone important might be hiding in your life? Jesus suggests that helping someone in need is just like helping him. During this month, look at a person you know as if they are Jesus.

2. Advent is intended to help us move from feelings of obligation and entitlement to feelings of anticipation and humility. When was a time that your anticipation of an event helped you appreciate it more? How can anticipation help you prepare your heart and mind?

3. As you think of incarnation as God putting on a body and walking with us, what are one or two ways that idea encourages you?

4. People wanted to be around Jesus, particularly at meals. What would it be like to anticipate eating a meal with Jesus? Would you be able to sit down, or would you be busy serving? What would you tell him as you were chatting at the table?

5. Read John 1:35-40. Who you are following in the way that Andrew and John were following John the Baptist? Who is giving you directions about how to change how you

live? This could be a trainer or pastor or advertiser or playwright or parent. How are they pointing you toward Jesus?

6. What's the best thing you ever had to drink? How did it change the way you looked at that beverage in the future? How did it change the way you looked at the person who served you? What would it be like to have food from Jesus?

7. Have you ever cheered for a team or a cause in spite of always being on the losing side? How did you stay encouraged? How would it encourage you if you knew that your cause would eventually win?

8. When is a time you saw someone care so much to defend the people they loved that they did something extraordinary or disruptive? How loved did it make the people being defended feel?

9. How many conversations do you think Jesus had that we don't know about? Conversations that were intended just for the one person rather than for everyone. How often does that still happen? Has it happened to you, now that you think about it?

10. Who have you known who has deferred to someone else with humility and intensity? How hard is it for you to deflect praise to the person who deserves it?

11. The story in John talks about tensions between Samaritans and Jews, men and women, living in marriage and not. How did Jesus pursue relationships across boundaries? What could you do to follow his model?

12. Delayed healing and pain are hard at the holidays. How can you be aware of the struggles of others during this season? How can you be willing to accept your own grief at this time?

13. The question Jesus asked the man at the fountain is the one we are still asked: "Do you want to get well?" What would you say to Jesus if he asked? What has been his

answer?

14. Is there a time that you have struggled with not measuring up to expectations around Christmas? What would it mean to think about expectancy, looking to the presence of Jesus?

15. Many of us can easily get caught up in performing for people rather than participating in life with them. What can you do that will help you be more participatory in Christmas celebrations this year?

16. How does it change our picture of God and of ourselves that Jesus actually lived in real places in Israel? Do you ever think about how tired Jesus would have been from a fifteen-mile hike in the hill country around Israel?

17. Where do you think John would be visiting people in your community? Where could you visit in ways that would show love for one another?

18. When have you been part of a miracle that you didn't recognize until it was done? How have you seen a small amount of food or words or time have influence beyond what would be expected?

19. Have you wondered what Jesus said in all of his times of teaching? What do you wish had been written down?

20. Although you may have never walked on water, how have you taken a step of faith toward Jesus? What's one that you have been waiting to take?

21. Have you ever wondered whether it was easier for people who saw Jesus to follow Jesus? How does it change your understanding of trusting him to know that people who touched him still didn't believe?

22. What are some of the ways that you think of Jesus? How can the way we see him change how we live our lives?

23. Have you ever listened to "All we like sheep?" You really should. What would restore your soul this week?

24. How can seeing Jesus as present in the ups and downs of our Christmas celebrations help us have courage to look

forward to the final resurrection?

25. Sometime on Christmas Day, reflect on how Advent has helped you prepare.

26. And now there are 364 days until Christmas. What are some of the ways you can carry a sense of anticipation through the year?

Acknowledgements

Nancy and I started walking together in 1982. Actually, taking walks in the streets of Wheaton, Illinois. On one of those walks, a week or two before our first date, we agreed to get married. When we renewed the practice of walking together in 2006, we had no idea how much the conversations would give us clarity and health and each other. And the setting for this book.

The readers of 300wordsaday.com met Saint John of the Mall the morning after I did, and welcomed him into their inboxes during Advent 2015 and 2016. As with all of my devotional writings, their presence and support draws me along.

The sustaining members of 300wordsaday.com provided underwriting for the publishing process. They also provided the encouragement that comes from someone financially investing in your words.

Paul Merrill has provided encouragement for years and designed the cover (pmerrill.com). Meg Hatch took the author's photo and the Hatch family has fed our hearts at their table (meghatchphotography.com).

And this project wouldn't have carried through without the affirmation of Char Binkley. She has been an example of faithful service to me and others for several decades. I think that John would enjoy talking with her very much.

About the author

Rev. Jon Swanson (PhD. The University of Texas) is a chaplain, author, educator, and consultant. After seventeen years in higher education and sixteen years as a pastor, he serves as a hospital chaplain, teaches spiritual formation and other pastoral courses for Bethel College (Indiana), and consults with congregations and nonprofits. He is author of *Lent for Non-Lent People* and *A Great Work*, which is a conversational commentary on Nehemiah. He writes daily meditations at 300wordsaday.com and has a regularly-growing online book about chaplaincy at BeforeYouWalkIn.com.

Jon and Nancy have been married since 1983 and have two adult, married children: Andrew (Allie) and Hope (Dan).

And they are still walking.

Made in the USA
Lexington, KY
08 December 2018